WISDOM OF INNOCENCE

A guide to children's perspective and self examination

By Michael J. Falcaro

ISBN: Softcover   978-1-5434-7692-7
       Hardcover   978-1-5434-7693-4
       EBook   978-1-5434-7691-0

Print information available on the last page

Rev. date: 10/17/2018

To order additional copies of this book, contact:
Xlibris
1-888-795-4274
www.Xlibris.com
Orders@Xlibris.com

DEDICATED TO: ABIGAIL A. FALCARO

As an adult without children, I thought I was confident in my perspective on many things. Then you came along and I began to question everything; you made me young again. While paying attention to your perspective and outlook on life, its made me question my view on many things and change for the better. Always examine yourself instead of others and never let anyone change who you are and what's important to you. Always be yourself and never stop loving and imagining.

Your Father,
Michael J. Falcaro

INTRODUCTION

I didn't write this for a long winded money maker or self interest portfolio builder; in-fact, I truly hope to take up the least amount of your time and hoped to articulate several key points in a minimal amount of words. Nothing is more valuable than time, and I certainly don't desire to waste anyone's, but rather utilize it by gaining valuable insight that will enrich both your relationship with your child or children and your own perspective of them and maybe even of yourself. I am no better of a parent than you or anyone else for that matter. I'm really not... however, I simply have had great success and happiness with building upon my children's confidence and imagination by heavily entrenching and involving myself, for which I truly hope I've been able to articulate in this micro book to help you. I wrote this because I care about you, who may be a stranger to me but is ultimately doing the most important duty in our society as well, which is raising future generations while doing it the best you can with what you have. We get this one short, fragile life where we have the ultimate responsibility of raising another human being that we are all deathly scared of doing. Collaborating with one another on what works is sometimes useless to some, but life changing to others; so all the more reason to offer what we can and lend a helping hand. After all, it takes a village.

My Dad often says that our "Children are our greatest teachers," which is incredibly true. My Mother often says "perception is reality," which is the very reason this book came to mind. After understanding perceptions outside my own with the help of a lot of humility, effort, and empathy, I began to witness a wisdom that's often overlooked or dismissed as I'm sure you do daily as well.

CHAPTER 1

PHILOSOPHICAL PRELUDE

It's commonly said, that the older we become, the more wisdom we obtain. The timeless saying "with age comes wisdom" has had this narrator not so convinced, ever since fatherhood. While being an adult, we tend to dismiss younger perspectives often because we believe that our experiences of hardships and longer life outweigh those who haven't endured as much life in general as we have. However, if someone hasn't experienced as many years as another, does that make them less wise in all aspects of life itself? Does wisdom really come with age? Or rather, does age taint one's perspectives as the years go by only to result in becoming more jaded and losing track of what's truly important or beautiful, or how to live life in general?

When having children, we presume that we know what's best in all aspects of life, or at the very least, we know better in comparison to the ones we ourselves are raising... and rightfully so, why would we ever think otherwise? We (the parents) are the grown-ups and full of life experience, and the children haven't been through what we have and don't know what we do. That being said, what if not going through as many heartaches and hardships as we have makes the child's perspective more important? What if not knowing what we do, doesn't make them know less than we do, but gives them untainted perspectives that differ from our possibly jaded ones?

As a society, we teach many things to our youth throughout their childhood and formal education but above all, we strive to encourage independence: Our goal is to get a child to stand on his or her own, think for himself or herself and be self sufficient. In order to get there, we teach them to question everything, be critical, and never stop learning. That being said, why wouldn't we, as adults, look back at our children for perspective to further our own? Perspective is a matter of perception and that continually changes throughout life; events, relationships, and so much more shape who we are, what direction we go in, what becomes important to us, and how we views things. In all actuality, how we are raised, our upbringing, and what we endure shapes the very fabric of who we are; which, in short, is our integrity. The egocentric part of who we are doesn't really make a child's perspective appealing for any adult to actually think that they have something to learn over someone who hasn't lived a fraction of the life they have. However, if we are able to get over ourselves with some possibly uncharted, modest humility, we might become more enlightened by perspective that we ourselves once held, but forgot about.

If perception is reality (which it is), to fully understand how or why we view things, we need to remember how we used to view things when our perspectives weren't jaded or altered with the harsh realities we've experienced. It's important to try to understand the how, the why and the what to truly comprehend our drift from a more innocent perspective. The remembrance is of the highest importance. How do we remember how we used to view anything and everything? It's impossible. As adults, we need to look at our children as teachers, just as we are to them. We can remember through their actions. Would a perception other than our own be that horrible to understand? If anything, it will enable us to the point of having empathy for what we failed to comprehend before; it will allow us to not only be on the same parallel wavelength as our children, but also expand our horizon of perspective. Moreover, becoming more in-tune to how a child sees, feels, and interacts with his or her surroundings, makes the adult that much more well-rounded and enlightened. Before taking initiative to better understand, we would simply make judgments, which is truly the easiest thing to do. Where in fact, the most difficult is to have empathy and before doing that, we truly need to get on the level of perspective and feel their senses, see their sight, understand their insight, and only then regardless of it making sense to our own reason, only then does our line of sight widen.

CHAPTER 2

INTEGRITY IS EVERYTHING

While becoming a parent, the stress of modeling a human being with proper structure, influence and upbringing is immeasurable. We simply do our best with what we have and as long as we truly put forth effort, show the affection, provide all the security, consistency, persistence, and above all, all of the love that we can; with all that and more, the child will be on his or her way through life. The substance that formulates that defines us on who we are, what's important to us, how we treat others is our integrity. As human beings we lose everything from respect to dignity over time but our integrity is the one thing we can always keep intact and hopefully never compromise, but rather build upon and enhance.

Our integrity has been tried, tested and shaped by many things, our moral outlook has been shaped, as well as our ethical decision making. Children's integrity is just as strong as an adults but where it lacks responsibility, reliability, dependability and so many things we've grown to obtain by earning credibility; theirs, on the other hand, is a sheer genuine untouched, unscathed outlook that will enhance our own enlightenment if incorporated and absorbed.

Children's integrity is of the most genuine. After enduring such trials, tribulations, and obstacles through life, we can only hope to return to such genuine full circle outlook as we have before becoming jaded throughout a society that projects such negativity. When coming full circle, understanding and respecting an outlook that lacks experience or simply differs from our own, we begin to not only tolerate outside perspectives but appreciate them as well.

An example of this is when one is entrenched among fellow adults and constantly bombarded with everyday issues stemming from politics to societal norms of constant judgments. One begins to feel the impact and weight of negativity and the toll it takes on one's own outlook. If one is around children and able to earnestly empathize with the child's thoughts, feelings, and perspectives, and then subsequently imitate or emulate the child when in the same aforementioned scenarios, one will realize the alleviation of stress and experience a more loving, accepting demeanor. For example, a child's innocence and pure outlook of acceptance and non judgment can and most certainly will better your own conversations with others from social concerns to the most controversial issues that create inevitable conflict. However, keeping empathy at the forefront of the conversations truly keeps it peaceful; peace can only start with empathy.

Having a genuine care for the person's opinion even if it differs from your own, keeps consistent respect in the fold of things and a child isn't quick to throw stones; nor do they feel the need/desire to be right over thy fellow person; neither should we. In doing this, it takes a huge amount of self restraint and content reminder of both empathy and humility to be applied before and after every comment and/or action... overtime self restraint won't even be needed because you'll simply grow to not only accept opposing views but love and respect them while agreeing to disagree. The older we get, the more fixated, narrow and stubborn we become but it doesn't have to be that way when we (ourselves) keep an open mind and never take ourselves too serious.

Children thrive in open environments that lack judgments, and enable them to think for themselves. They need guidance but above all, they need the ability to find themselves and become independent. To reiterate the process of formulating themselves and finding out who they are; their priorities, how they view and treat others (their integrity) they do it with the most genuine perspective because they simply don't know it all and neither do we. Children ask questions, we should never cease to try to answer them and ask them of ourselves. Sometimes taking a step back and asking them questions for a change is helpful. Questions of all kinds, questions about how they view anything and everything because it will in-fact differ from your own answers; it doesn't make our answers right or wrong from their own--just a different, and very interesting, perception. These continual questions are more helpful than you know; not only does it help you know your child as you are privy to his or her personal thoughts, but it also enriches the bond you have as well as their own sense of self importance because his or her words matter and are a priority to you. Moreover, Socrates said it best, "question everything." Children do this naturally; they're trying to experience and understand the world around them. As parents, however, we fall under "everything" that should be questioned; therefore, why are we ever bothered by being questioned by our children or hassled to take the time to explain things in detail to them. Our reaction of being questioned should be with enthusiasm because it only shows their independence and willingness to learn and should be handled with patience. Moreover, if we (ourselves) desire true change and are constantly evolving like our children are doing each and everyday under our care and guidance, we need to question everything about ourselves and show true courage by making this a change for not only our own betterment but of our children.

Too often as we grow into and later reach adulthood, we stop asking questions and lose track of humility and sometimes learning in general; that's what separates the perspective of kids to adults. Children know they don't know it all and have humility as a part of their everyday character while we as adults many times let humility fall to the wayside in that regard. We lose track of humility either out of how it may look to others if asking questions, fear of looking vulnerable or weak or ignorant. Most of the time, our inability to look in the mirror and make a change stems from our own arrogance and short sighted perspective and lack of desire to broaden or enhance our own perception. Nevertheless, the separation doesn't need to exist. The enlightenment of an adult can be far greater than ever before if we don't lose track of what makes children young, genuine, and pure. The mindset of youth has little to do with age; it's the desire and willingness to learn and not judge. To earnestly care about yourself enough to become better than we were every day that follows. Instead of becoming jaded from societal norms we are all forced at times to lose or give up on our idealistic mindset, children have wonder in their minds and in their hearts always; which truly makes them see the world in every way. We can maintain such amazing attributes, just like our children, that enrich our own mind, body and soul--ones that are worthy of emulation and enrich our own happiness. We simply have to reignite the innocence that we all once had by putting forth an open mind and closing the prejudices and biases that handicap us from evolving.

If we can keep our mindset with love at the forefront coupled with empathy, humility, and curiosity, our children will notice it and thrive on it. We instantly become more appealing and relatable to our children. Our personalities, personas, and interactions will intrigue and attract our children's attentions and our relations will only enhance as a result. Children immediately begin to flock in our direction when we interact because they won't fear being judged and they will feel comfortable and listened to. Our perception becomes more attuned with theirs with open-mindedness, suspense of disbelief, and positive outlooks, which most people in general are naturally attracted to.

CHAPTER 3

ENVIRONMENT OF INVOLVEMENT

There's nothing more important than time with one's own children. After all, we only have such limited time before our children want to do their own things while in those teenage years and then become adults very soon after. Nothing is more valuable than time because no other commodity is more precious and limited, and our children appreciate and deserve our "spent time" with them above all other things. Time itself is taken for granted and isn't appreciated or missed until its shortened, passed, or run out. If we really live in the moment and spend our time wisely, we have to prioritize it while we spend it right now. In today's society, we don't have to look far to witness content neglect while seeing parents engrossed in their phones while their children sit across from them either doing the same or simply desiring their parents' attention. If the gizmos or gadgets aren't there to carry their attention, our children are lost and seek attention that they often are not getting. It is far more healthy to simply talk rather than text and wrestle around instead of playing video games, hold hands and take a walk instead of having them play with a toy by themselves.

While getting on a child's level, one may become discouraged overtime due to not being able to relate and/or fully understand the comprehension of how the child viewed things in his or her spectrum. Try not to be discouraged, as the goal is to find enlightenment through a child's perception little by little by empathizing and learning and not trying to know them completely because then we would proclaim ourselves as know it all's and that we are changing about ourselves the most in this process. Instead of becoming amused of children's actions and reactions in comparison to our own and shrugging it off and saying things like "kids say the darndest things" or "out of the mouth of babes", but rather actually take the time to understand them through the eyes of the beholder. Too often throughout our society parents simply talk at their children

10

rather than with them and simply don't have conversations with them regularly and instead continue with authoritative relationships with their children. This is certainly an error in our society's thinking and as a result, an error in our parenting. Kids need social interaction but they need your attention more than anything. Not your attention for their amusement, not gifts or favors for their brief happiness, but rather your undivided attention and focus to simply engage with them in meaningful dialogue.

This transparency must be frequent and consistent not only through the week but each and every day. We want to continually build that good rapport with them, and one way to do this is to give them the attention that they are seeking. When our kids enter a room, we can show a little excitement even if we just saw them an hour prior; their need to feel special never turns into a void if it's simply fulfilled, so we need to make the effort to engage them whenever possible. These efforts don't need to be these grandiose actions; in fact, it's the small, frequent, consistent actions that will enable them to feel secure in their environment.

The more we communicate with our children, the more they will open up with their own perspective on things to us that we should never belittle, dismiss, or discourage, no matter how silly or arbitrary they may seem. Kids, especially younger children, see the world vastly different than adults. And so they should. It doesn't make it less real than the way we see things; only the perception is different for which we should continuously strive to understand. Nevertheless, plunge away and don't stray from the course. Know it is far more rewarding and healthy to gain additional perspective other than your own in every aspect of life; especially how we view it (life itself) in general. When we notice these vastly different perceptions, this is when we need to ask our children questions about anything and everything in hopes of gaining their perspective; doing this also builds our children's sense of self worth and confidence and enhances our relationships our children. If your child likes superheroes, ask why; they might be lacking the ability to do something themselves that they desire or lack a role model in their lives or simply have a void of some kind… if they get emotional over a song or movie or picture or when you say something to them, ask why, talk a lot and listen more and above all, be patient. Another example is if something angers you child either it be an action, interaction or involvement of some kind, be patient and remember your child fragile state of mind and lack of coping abilities. Throughout this process, one's own patience and humility is essential and no task is too silly and time consuming. Humility in general is one of the greatest virtues to possess and arguably most rare and lacking in our current society. If humility isn't obtained, people will never see their children's perspective as worth understanding; nor would they ever see wisdom in a child while being an adult and remain an authoritative figure carrying out their responsibilities and nothing more.

Providing an environment of involvement is so important for a child's sense of confidence and self worth. Feeling included and the enjoyment of others taking part in what they enjoy is all that much better. Even if the child wants to just play with his or her toys, that's fine, but play with them. No matter how silly it seems, pick up a toy, figure, or whatever and attempt a different voice for it and build a story with it along with which toy they are playing with. If the setting is different, and it's a dance floor for an example and you're child is doing some sort of corky, wavy, wiggling wacky dance, try it out yourself. If you're worried about onlookers or how you're viewed, don't worry yourself, it's a perfectly normal fear. That being said, we are always going to care about judgments, but we have to thicken our skin for the sake of our children because their judgments matter more than anyone else's. If someone mistakes your kindness, or in this case goofiness, for weakness, that's a reflection on their character, not yours. Sometimes doing something outside your normal interaction/involvement can be uncomfortable and even fearful. Napoleon Bonaparte said, "he who fears being conquered is sure of defeat." In other words, even if it's just a simple dance or skip in front of others, do it with confidence and reassurance that with no risk, there's no rewards, and if you feel silly, don't because you're stronger in that moment for that child through their perception than you'll ever be perceived by anyone else. Besides, if someone judges you harshly or unfairly, it's to be expected; instead of people empathizing or trying to relate or admire, it far easier to simply judge, especially while the person themselves aren't happy with their own predicament and/or self perception, so be mindful that misery loves company and then go in the opposite direction.

To reiterate, you being the child's parent are viewed not only as their authority or disciplinarian figure but also as more of a superhero than you know, so why would you care what anyone else thinks of you but them? If you hold your little girl's hand and skip the whole way through a parking lot to get to the grocery store, she will be imprinted with that memory and feeling of happiness for a lifetime. If you act like a robot or fictitious superhero for your son's imagination or even amusement, your son will be imprinted with the happiness and bonding. The only person that you should be focused on is the child. People are going to talk and may even make faces but what matters is the smile on your child's face, and how your child perceives you. If you're willing to throw caution in the wind and dance up a storm with moves that teenagers would think are foul and "just ain't right" because you don't have rhythm, it's wonderful because you do have your child's attention and that's all that matters.

It's all about more than just entertaining your child. It's the amount of involvement you can provide while you can during the short time you have with them. Throughout a vast lifetime, even as adults, they are looking to you as their role model, hero, guide, etc. It's important to enable the best environment to enhance their childhood for the short time they have it. Moments of carefree devotion you do for them is what cements your legacy as his or her hero for life.

It's not the big monumental achievements or events that are always heavily anticipated but rather, the collection of small moments that culminate over time that pass us day after day and night after night that define relationships between us and our children. We create the environments through our interaction and involvements which forms their perceptions. That alone means the world to kids; not only playing with them but taking the initiative to allocate time for them as well as doing so building upon their imaginative setting. Remember: Just because we grew out of our childhood, doesn't mean we can't help the betterment of someone else's.

Children themselves prefer involvement over objects being bought, goods, services, or tasks carried out for them. Instead, the more interactive you are and initiative you take to be with them, the more valued and grateful they will be. Objects and stuff in general are nice to have and provide, but it isn't the way to a loved one's heart or even admiration; it is sincere persistence and earnest intentions of desired spent time with them. Overtime, one's own perception of their child can and will transcend from them being fragile and naive to a more strong positive outlook that simply differs from your own. Children's perception and mindset nearly always differs from your own but should never dismissed; moreover, it should be respected and supported. Instead of constantly directing, controlling and managing our children by dictating behaviors, it's important to never take a back seat but a side seat approach and enjoy the ride with them. Ask questions as much/if not more so than they do and patiently understand what's important to them and why and never judge it poorly regardless of your thoughts.

CHAPTER 4

PARENTING IS IMPRESSIONABLE

As time goes on, while being constantly involved, relationships will undoubtedly grow stronger than most and many around you will notice. At the forefront of interaction and involvement with your child, never project your own prejudice or bias purposely on a subject matter--not even the slightest remark "eww" to a snake or bug; your child might say how beautiful it is before taking in account how we perceive it. Regardless how off the wall their perceptions may or may not be towards something, always positively enforce their views, opinion and perception, as long as it's not harmful in any way shape or form.

Negative reinforcement happens too often throughout our society. The words we speak are more powerful than we think; not to mention the action we do or don't do in some cases. Everything is subjected to be judged, assessed, and mimicked. Above all, our reaction to them will hold weight on their conscience. We, as the adults, have to hold back and evaluate so carefully to not poison their minds with a jaded society that often poisons our own. Try to never condemn actions, beliefs and opinions of subject matter that holds innocence in their eyes. For example, no matter how annoying a purple singing dinosaur is or dancing wiggly characters are to adults after a hard day's work, just know your children's enjoyment and perception can easily be altered by the slightest off hand comment of annoyance. Their childhood heros or just favorite shows and interests of any kind can crumble from a mere comment from whom they admire moreso--you. Furthermore, to emphasize how powerful words, actions, and inactions are to a child's sponge-like mind, always remember all behavior is learned behavior. From actions of smoking a cigarette to inactions of not holding a door open for a lady or simply tensing up when around various ethnic or social groups that differ from your own. Most jaded perspectives and even prejudices are learned from influences that are directly and indirectly transcended to the child from our own behaviors.

Just like the laws, cause and effect actions are just as important as reactions, so always take anything and everything with a loving response. After all, children are impressionable and everything from thoughts of theirs to beliefs can change from a simple comment like "there's no such thing," "grow up already," or just "get real." Some would make the argument that allowing a child to believe in Santa is lying, but those arguments come from people who simply lost their suspense of disbelief; which is all you need to enjoy a good movie, make the best out of a fairytale, or think of the world in different aspects other than what we are programmed to find "normal" and "acceptable" in everyday society. Suspending our stubborn sense of believability allows our imagination to set sail and your child will notice and enjoy the journey with you more so when you (yourself) aren't critical or a naysayer.

Moreover, too often in our society we hear the phrase "aren't you a little old for that?" which truly is one of the worst things to say to a child. It makes them not only embarrassed but at times ashamed for what they are doing, and it makes them rethink their action that brings them enjoyment as childish and not to be taking part in; this is one more step away from their inner child. Who are we (or anyone) to say what's "age appropriate"? Our society is incredibly "label happy." we have age labels on toys, activities and even label our own children if they learn differently than others. Everything is labeling and in all actuality, if you label anyone, you negate them entirely. If a teenager wants to trick-or-treat or an adult wants to play with army men, who is anyone to deem what's socially acceptable or "age appropriate." Directly or indirectly speaking out against something that brings laughter or enjoyment will slowly but surely force children to grow up, and there is no reason to rush that process. Words are powerful and coming from a parent, who is most impressionable on them, makes them rethink their actions and enjoyments. If they aren't hurting anyone or themselves, one should be supportive and be positive towards it and hopefully even take part.

Aside from what's said out loud verbally, the actions we take, don't take, and even our reactions are arguably the most important because of the energy we put out. When your child enters a room, whether he or she is enthusiastically greeted from your genuine excitement of his or her company, or if he or she simply acknowledged of for his or her existence, it has a huge impact on the relationship and association the child will have with you. In short, it's all about your mood. We all have been in the scenarios of laughter, happiness, or celebratory happenings and that one person comes in the room either negatively or miserably and sucks the life out of the room. We all absorb people's energy in one way or another; we are affected directly or indirectly but we really are all interconnected. Children will pick up on your mood faster than most because they are the most affected by it because they are not only more in-tuned but more impressionable. Kids are sponges and mimic behaviors and react to them even if nothing is said or done. Non-verbal communication is far more than 80% of communication in general and simple moods, attitudes, and energy. What we put out is what they respond to the most. Hence, if you're in a bad mood, mask that mood so it doesn't have to be theirs. Remember, it's not about you; since you had a child, it's about them. Remember even more importantly, that you're only going to have this child for a short amount of time because it does go fast. How you mask the mood is up to a whole different author, who knows a lot more than this one in regard to channeling energy, but my own suggestions are hit a punching bag, yell in a pillow (never at your child), go the the gym, or better yet, simply talk to someone. The one thing our human species does the most is the one thing we all need to learn to do better, and that's communicate.

That being said, attempting to constantly and continuously shield your child from negativity is seemingly impossible, so trying to do so is a recipe for disaster; all that's needed is effort on your part because realistically, they will ultimately be exposed to outside negativity, but hopefully through your encouragement and reinforcement of who they are and the confidence they'll obtain due to your involvement, the negative doses will not have any consequence as you will have enabled them to remain themselves if they are strong-willed enough and supported by you. After you grow supportive of your child's perception and take part in it too, it becomes that much more enjoyable for them to be themselves and let you in. You're seen in their eyes in more diverse ways than you were before; now you're someone they can comfortably interact with without having a metaphorical wall of any kind and openly converse without fear of judgment. Kids can be kids, knowing that you're a kid at heart and they won't feel silly to simply imagine or dare to dream in front of you, but rather, they'll collaborate and elaborate those thoughts and feelings even more so with you.

Taking part in an open mindset that's traditionally not your own can feel uncomfortable and even unsettling at times because if we're true to ourselves, we know we simply don't know how to be something that we are not used to. However, when becoming both loving and humble enough to subject yourself to others perceptions, outside your own, like watching a film or reading fiction, we need to suspend our disbelief. Even if something to do with your child, either it be playing with a figurine while using a different voice or imagining something being vastly different than it really is like a broom being a princess or however it looks from onlookers even if you think it's at your expense, you begins to retain a more positive outlook just like the child possesses.

Adults who simply spend more time with children find themselves more compassionate about things and sensitive about the harsh judgments of society for which we are all subjected and plagued with daily, whether it be gender or racially fueled or superficially or socially charged comments, we all hear them. Just know things like difference in skin color or what's cool and what's not are learned behaviors that are taught; all of which have huge impressions on a child's perspective. Not only does every action help shape your child but reactions do as well. An excellent quote to keep at the forefront of every reaction in regards to your child, whether they accidentally hit you somewhere and the pain becomes unbearable or they break something unimaginable, the pain is (hopefully) temporary and the possession is just a material that you can't take with you when you pass, so resight and remember this throughout everything: "People will forget what you said, People will forget what you did, but people will never forget how you made them feel" (Eleanor Roosevelt). Children will always remember how you make them feel, always.

CHAPTER 5

EVOLVING AS A SPECIES

When change takes place, real change, it's scary and one of the hardest things to do is to not only accept change, because after all, we are all creatures of habit, but to bring forth change ourselves. We need to take the initiative to simply humble ourselves to the idea that we are no better than anyone else and vice-versa, and we're all just different. The same principle applies to children. Self examination is truly a healthy practice for any adult, but with regards to parenting, it's essential! One needs to constantly examine his or her own actions and make changes.... because children are watching. Making judgments while looking in the mirror is the toughest task but most rewarding, for it is said, "The unexamined life isn't worth living" (Plato).

Never try to be a better man/woman than anyone else; those are just insecurities and egocentric thoughts that lead to narcissism. Instead, strive to always be better than the person you were yesterday. Taking an active role of intrigue and initiative to enable our inner child's imagination makes imagining all the more creative and interactive with your own child and will change your own spectrum to say the least. If we aren't always trying to evolve and change for our own betterment, what's the point of anything? What are we doing but only wasting away then? See a prism of ideas outside your own, imaginative and creative thoughts and beauty in things you'd not otherwise think as beautiful until understanding the mind of innocence; only then can we begin to see wisdom in children.

Everyday, find yourself both teaching and learning from your children. In time you'll find out that your children will be among your greatest of teachers. When we begin to put our egos aside, only then we begin to appreciate and see value in our childrens unscaved and unbias perceptions throughout life; which is nothing short of inspiring at times… Their energy is always positive and enthusiastic and never jaded with any prejudice that society showers daily. Instead of sheltering and controlling every situation with your child (which is impossible to begin with) try to empower your child daily by asking continual questions of what they believe, how do they see things and why??? Valuing their perception is paramount to bonding relations with you child and once we get over ourselves and realize it's not about us; but rather them, we enjoy the ride much more riding with them in everyday life, rather than for them. Granted, we are the ones who are in-charge of modeling for them and not vice-versa, but a good parent knows that too much sheltering is simply not healthy. One of the scariest things of parenting is the balancing act of what we don't want to do but knows its best for them… giving a child space is a prime example of this. At the risk of sounding corny, space a frontier that children need at times. As much as we may want to smother them or always interact with them, space is what he or she needs in order to find themselves, in regards to their own interests, passions, likes, dislikes etc, in life. Why not take part in a constructive sense and never oppress their views but rather uplift them with encouragement? After all, it's not about us anymore. After a few years (that will go incredibly quickly), they leave the nest, and you can take part in the selfie era as much as the next person but while you have this person who will think of you as a superhero your entire life, you should try not to disappoint.

Dream and imagine with them and let them guide your hand just as much as you guide theirs. Every moment we get, it's time passed, and if not appreciated to its fullest, we're simply not living; but rather cheating valued time and precious life. It's so short and fragile, it should always be cherished in the present. So that being said, please think of every moment with your child is one day closer for their childhood coming to a halt, so while living in the present, we need to humble ourselves and suspend disbelief and allow their genuine, open-minded and loving perception affect our own while we encourage and build upon their creativity and imagination for not only their betterment but for yours as well. If we take for granted the youth among us by putting off the best we can be day after day due to effort it takes, we not only cheat the childhood your child could be having, but we also cheat ourselves. If we are actively take part in our child's innocent perception and allow it to sink into our own trying to be better every day after the next, we can truly proclaim enlightenment and evolution as we make moments cherished memories before they pass us by.

Be both assertive as the parent and sensitive; it's essential to juggle/manage both to carry the child's respect and admiration. Throughout it all combined with empathy, humility and loving attention it all must be with consistent involvement. Children are our future and the only real legacy we leave this world, so it's only right that they feel a sense of importance due to our devotion and interest in them. With age can come wisdom but please know that youth has wisdom that we all lose overtime--it's wisdom that we forget and can't even relate to, let alone rationalize, but since when does wisdom have to be rational? Through proper prioritization of time spent allocated interaction towards our children, who deserve nothing less than being our top priorities, we regain perspective, belief, and a more optimistic, positive and pure perspective that will enhance our own health and social outlook and most importantly our relationships with our children. To reiterate and emphasize, when spending time with our children on their level, their innocence becomes infectious and their spectrum will coincide with our own and truly contribute to bonding and happiness. Children's wisdom of innocence truly enhances our worldly outlook on everyone and everything for our own betterment. If we simply step aside, but never away, and actually listen to kids, instead of just hearing them, our children become our greatest teachers that enable us to be more youthful, imaginative, empathetic, and loving, and we can keep our children genuine and almost magical to an outsider's perspective. An adult can be just as enthusiastic about life as a child, everything can be loving and valuable and never taken for granted. Wisdom, when unscaved and at its purest form, is a beauty like no other and an everlasting positive perspective that will undoubtedly keep you and your child forever young together.

That being said, the old adage that "with age comes wisdom" is not the case; true wisdom is a core characteristic of genuine perspective upheld with empathy, humility, and many other attributes that we tend to lose overtime that change our mindset and outlook of the world. To be be innocent has nothing to do with number of years lived or experiences achieved or endured; we can adopt such principled perception and begin to turn back our own metaphorical clocks of inner peace by not allowing jaded individuals infect negativity on us due to being unhappy themselves and lack integrity themselves. We as a society need to stop talking at our children and begin to talk with them and never underestimate them. We can learn from them if we allow ourselves to. How we see the world is an accurate reflection of our own happiness that hinders our capacity to live, laugh, and love while we can and with whom we can. We are capable of loving so much more than we do. We are capable of so much more happiness than we allow ourselves. Aside from humility, it only takes knowledge of one's own self over selfies and empathy over egos and interactive patient effort while parenting to drive along side your child for the ride of a better lifetime with one another.

EPILOGUE

My inspiration for writing this book is my daughter, Abigail. At first, I was amused by her cute and auspicious view on the simplest things. The more I paid attention and contemplated her thoughts and opinions on whatever the matter at hand, the more I began to examine the depth of her insights. For your own contemplation, I've included a few of my favorites along with some candid pictures of her during each experience. Only "Out of the mouths of babes" can such simple and sometimes obvious wisdom be imparted. Those thoughts, feelings, and actions are more than just "kids say and do the darndest things" as we all often simplify without actually giving thought towards it. While taking time to understand a child's perception, it can enhance our own perspective in and on all matters. Children's innocent perspective is has more wisdom than you'll ever understand unless you try; that being said, what do you have to lose when so much can be gained, after all, they are worth the time, effort, and energy.

Wisdom from the Innocence of my Abigail:

Abigail: (Abbie wore these several days in a row), when I asked her why she was wearing them all the time, she indicated "Everything's better seeing it in Pink".

This picture is me giving Abbie space and allowing her own moments of reflection to occur.

Abbie telling her Smurfs "God made you the way you are and you're all beautiful and we're having fun"

Abbie: "These worms are so beautiful. They are just beautiful. They are my friends."

Her Dad: (I didn't let my perception of worms being gross show and simply responded) "Oh, that's beautiful hunny"

Abbie has moments with all living beings as depicted in the two images above where she has a special connection with a donkey that she just met at her Uncle's farm.

While visiting a shelter, Abbie couldn't help but notice the sadness of a puppy; who she had to take home and named her Olive.

Where many people would turn a blind eye to this puppy, seeing so many others that are "cuter", Abbie fell in love and convinced her parents to save Rosie, who had many health problems but has progressed greatly since and is very happy & loved.

Abbie is seen here watering her garden which consists of weeds, but to her, all living things are valuable and precious.

Abigail: (This is a good depiction of Abbie showing love without prejudice while many others would be frightened by her puppy's appearance.)

Abigail: "Circles are the best because they never end"

Me: I'll Never forget this and never underestimating her or any other child for that matter.

Printed in the United States
By Bookmasters